The Return of Christ ...

What If

1/3/12

Carol,

May our Lord Jesus
bless you as you watch
& prepare for His return.
Blessings to you & yours.

For His Glory,

Dolce L. Inzerillo

2 Tim 2:15
KJV
Rev 16:15

D.R. Inzerillo

Unless otherwise noted, all scriptures are taken from the *Holy Bible, King James Version* of the Bible, © 1976 by Thomas Nelson, Inc.

Other Reference Material are Listed as Follows:
The New Strong's Exhaustive Concordance of the Bible, James Strong, Copyright © 1995, 1996
Webster's Dictionary, Copyright © 1976

Published by: D. R. Inzerillo
Cover Photo: ©iStockphoto.com/Zhuravlov Igor V., Photographer
Back Cover Design: Deborah Gardner
Editing by: A. Barken, D. R. Inzerillo

ISBN # 978-0-615-41349-5

Dedication

Since my Lord and Savior, Jesus Christ, gave this book to me, I first dedicate it back to Him.

Next, I dedicate this book to my devoted husband Joe and our three treasured children: Jordan (who is already home with Jesus), Jacob, and Caleb; "Merm", "Pops" (also with Jesus), "Craigers" and "Neaner"; those who are seeking to know the Lord; and to those that by faith have already come to know Jesus as their Lord and Savior.

May we all study to show ourselves approved as we watch, pray, and prepare for His mighty return, that we may have eternity together with Him.

I give you my heart, my love, and God's truth.

Acknowledgements

First and foremost, I thank my Lord, Jesus Christ. Publishing this book just goes to show you that God uses ordinary people to do extraordinary things for His Glory and Kingdom.

To my husband and our boys, who graciously supported my efforts and gave me lots of "get-a-way time" to accomplish God's task, I give my love and ask for an abundance of blessings upon them.

Recognizing my B & B study partner and treasured friend Aida, my heartfelt thanks and deep appreciation for all your faithful prayers, support, accountability, dedication, encouragement, and fun through this long exhilarating journey of discovering God's truth together.

To many precious friends who helped along the way, prayed, encouraged, loved me through the valleys, and ushered in wise counsel, you know who you are, I am deeply grateful. You will never know this side of heaven, the impact you have made in my heart.

In order to reach the end, there must be a beginning. What's in-between those two vital steps is where a select few (Eugene, Brenda, Kirk, Ted, Kelly, Scott and others) contributed their valuable time and talents, to which I extend my genuine gratitude.

Truly a team effort and with all sincerity, "Thank you." I ask and trust our Lord Jesus to bless us all for our obedience to Him.

The Return of Christ...
What If

Table of Contents

Getting Ready for the Grand Finale

There are many different views, "interpretations" if you will, about the return of Christ. The purpose of this book is to encourage and *challenge* you to dig deeper into God's Word, therefore, finding HIS answers - not man's opinion (2 Tim 2:15; Acts 5:29; 1 Cor 2:1-5; 1 John 2:27). "Study to shew thyself approved unto God ..." (2 Tim 2:15 KJV).

As many thought provoking questions are asked and scriptures referenced, my prayer for you is that you sit with the Lord, having an open mind to listen and see what His Word tells you - putting aside previous thoughts, teachings and wishful hopes that possibly may have been misrepresented. Just allow the Holy Spirit to guide you to a deeper understanding of His truth. I also encourage you to look up the scriptures. A pastor once told me if you study, research and dig deep into God's Word, not only will God reveal His truth but "... ye need not that any man teach you ..." (1 John 2:27) and no one will be able to take it away from you because you studied, you did the work, you learned His truth.

It will help you to read this book in its entirety first before referencing the scriptures. I encourage you to then go back and read it a second or third time and look up the scriptures in the King James Version (KJV) of the Bible. When reviewing scripture, compare the KJV to others. In some instances, you may be quite surprised how just a slight difference in the translation has a significant impact on the meaning of God's Word. Read and compare. Notice how God rarely tells us something only once. He tells us, shows us, time and again. Keep in mind, God is the same yesterday, today, and tomorrow (Heb 13:8; Ps 102:27; Mal 3:6; James 1:17).

For purposes of not wanting to get too lengthy, some words or items are used in a general sense so please don't let this distract you. Let's focus on the bigger picture. For example, when referring to "tribulation," I'm referring to the seven year period described in The Book of Daniel as the 70th week. When using the word "pretrib rapture" or "pretribulation", I'm referring to a period of time either before the Seven Year Tribulation starts or just at the onset, the beginning perhaps, of that seven year period. When using the word "rapture" which technically isn't in the Bible, the word "Easter" isn't either for that matter, there are other events, episodes, even doing word studies, which help clarify and describe these or other words that are more commonly used today. "Rapture" here is used to describe the event when Christ comes back to get us, His church, the believers. Let's not get hung up on the technicalities, but understand the general concept or direction of the questions being asked and what we need to consider ... let's see God's bigger picture.

Imagine, if you will, what it must have been like for Noah ... knowing what's to come, seeing and living amongst the wickedness of the world, as he steps out in faith and builds the ark. (This I might add was no small task. The ark was not only immense, it was absolutely gigantic for their time, measuring 450 feet long (or 150 yards), that's 1 ½ football fields, 75 feet wide and 45 feet high. ~ Gen 6:12-18) Noah telling, warning, trying to help anyone who would listen ... and for 120 years ... going through ridicule and rejection, being made fun of, then ... the rain comes, which they had never seen before, the doors of the ark close ... and as he hears the terrifying screams of those who refused to listen, refused to repent, refused to obey. Noah and his family are reminded that they are under God's protection, and rewarded for Noah's obedience and faithfulness.

God's Word tells us to beware of many false teachings and deceptions, especially in the last days. The

Bible also tells us that as Christians, we will endure much suffering, we will be tested and tried, refined like gold, and that we are to **share in the suffering** in order to share in His glory. (1 Pet 1:6-7; Rom 8:17; Phil 1:29-30, 3:7-11; 2 Tim 3:12; 2 Cor 4:7-11, 11:16-32; 1 Thes 3:1-5; 2 Thes 1:15; Acts 9:15-16; Zech 13:8-9...)

Besides the many warnings of deceptions, trials and testing to come, we are **commanded** to watch and to prepare ("take heed"- Matt 24, 25:1-13; Mark 13; Luke 21; 1 Thes 5:6). Since it's a command, do you think we should pay attention? Knowing what they know now, if the people of Noah's day got a "do-over," do you think they'd heed the call, watch and prepare? Bringing it back to today, what are we to watch and prepare for? Do you think God would instruct us to watch then not tell us what to watch for ... and why ... and how to prepare?

Before we dig deeper together, let's play the "what if" game. "What if" we are raptured up with/to the Lord before the seven years of Tribulation? What would we be watching and preparing for? What would be the point? Why the command to do so? "What if" we aren't raptured out before the Seven Year Tribulation, but perhaps we have to go through some or all of it? "What if" we have to endure more trials and tests (tribulations)? Would that be

12

reason enough to need to watch and prepare? Would it be important to you to know what to watch for ... how and why to be prepared? "What if" you don't watch and aren't prepared? Think there might be a chance you could be deceived by the enemy? Where would you turn? How will you know what is coming next? If you are screaming, running, and terrified like those left in the flood, how can you stand still and know God ... and know with confidence how His plan plays out?

Rehearsals are imperative for performances. The only way to rehearse (practice) is to know the script and get the training under the Author and/or Director of the play. God has given us the play, His script. He tells us to study, to prepare, to watch, and what to watch for so that we may be ready for the program, the grand finale, Christ's return. I encourage you to continue studying, dig even deeper for His truths, and get ready. After all, it's your eternity that's at stake here.

The next several pages bring up some important questions to consider no matter what your "end times" beliefs are. They also point to much of God's Word to think about, pray through, and apply.

Again, I strongly urge you to read all the way through the book in its entirety to get God's bigger picture before stopping to look up specific scripture (not necessarily reading the entire book in one sitting mind you). Upon your second or third reading, I encourage you to then look up scripture. For your convenience, "Study Notes" have been added at the back of the book.

Now let's take a look together at what the Bible says.

Are Tribulation and Wrath the Same?

Some believe tribulation and wrath are one in the same. Let's play the "what if" game again. What if tribulation and wrath have the same meaning, interpretation, definition, how does that line up with God's Word? Let's see ... God's Word says, "... for God has not appointed us to wrath" (us being His believers, 1 Thes 5:9) and He will "keep thee from the hour of temptation" (Rev 3:10). But what exactly does "keep thee from the hour of temptation" mean (Rev 3:10)? Well, when doing a word study, you will see "the hour" in "keep thee from the hour of temptation" (Rev 3:10) refers to the hour of wrath (Rev 18:10, a specific allotment of time, seven years of tribulation with one hour of wrath). If tribulation and wrath are the same, we could make the following conclusions: Per the scriptures above, we can't be here for <u>any</u> of the seven year tribulation/wrath; therefore, we are raptured pretrib. Hmm! We know there is a seven year period still to come, "the Tribulation." Why then, with all of God's believers raptured out of here, would God take seven more years to cleanse the earth? What's the purpose? This directly contradicts God's Word which says it will come upon them as "sudden destruction" (1 Thes 5:2-3, the flood, Sodom and Gomorrah).

Something else to think about ... God's Word says we will be coming back in a twinkling of an eye (1 Cor 15:52). So if we are raptured then return in a twinkling of an eye, what's to come back to? God is bringing sudden destruction so there won't be an earth as we know it to come back to. But wait! There is still seven more years of tribulation left for those left behind. How can that be? Didn't they die in God's sudden destruction? Yet all have up to the fifth vial to repent (Rev 16:10-11) and the seven years of Tribulation is just beginning. There are still **seven** seals, **seven** trumpets, and **seven** vials to go. Maybe we come back celestial, as the Word says (1 Cor 15:52), but hang out for those seven years? What sense would that make? What would be the purpose? We'd still go through the tribulation would we not? Then what? Does Christ come back a third time and get us yet again? Where in scripture does it back that up? If tribulation and wrath are the same event, praise the Lord (PTL) no watching, no preparing, no trials, no testing, no intense suffering, no enduring, no overcoming ... Cool !!! PTL!!! We are home, end of story!

What if tribulation and wrath are two separate events with completely different meanings and purposes? How does that line up with scripture?

Researching the Bible (KJV), Strong's Concordance, and Webster's Dictionary, resulted in the following definitions and purposes:

✠ <u>Definition and Purpose of "Tribulation"</u>

Definition: trials, testing.

Purpose: "... your faith ... may be proven genuine and may result in praise, glory and honor when Jesus Christ is revealed." (1 Pet 1:6-7; 4:12-19; Rom 8:17; Jas 1:2-4, 12) Tribulation is a seven year period of time <u>the world</u> will pass through to include conditions causing distress, affliction, suffering, persecution, oppression (Deut 4:30; Ps 66:10-12; Dan 11:35; Matt 24:21, 29; Mark 13:24; John 16:33; Acts 14:22; Rom 8:35; 1 Thes 3:3-4; 2 Thes 1:4; 2 Tim 3:12; Jas 1:2-4; Rev 2:10, 3:10). The Seven Year Tribulation period has yet another purpose ... to get the Jews on board.

✠ <u>Definition and Purpose of "Wrath"</u>

Definition: destruction, destroy, divine punishment for an offense or crime.

Purpose: To punish/destroy the wicked, those not choosing to follow/obey God. Wrath is God's personal anger resulting in ending, changing, the world as we know it (Isa 30:27-33; Luke 21:23; Eph 5:6; Col 3:6; Heb 3:6, 11; 2 Thes 1:8-10; 2 Pet 2:4-10; Rev 6:17, 11:18, 12:12, 12:17, 19:15. A word study on "wrath" leads to studies on anger, enrage, violent, fury, fierce ... they come full circle back to wrath, destruction).

Knowing all have an awareness of God (Rom 1:20; Col 1:23), do you think anyone knowingly choosing <u>not</u> to accept Jesus and obey God would qualify as "an offense or crime" to God, therefore, resulting in the consequence of wrath?

Let's go back to God's Word for a moment. In an earlier example, it was pointed out "... for God has not appointed us to wrath" (1 Thes 5:9). Hmm, what do you suppose appointed means? Let's think about that for a moment. Let's say I had an appointment at the doctor's and I invited you to come along. Would it be your appointment? No! It's my appointment. Could you come, sit in, listen, observe, and even ask questions perhaps, even though it's not your appointment? Of course you could. Just because it's not our appointment, we believers, that doesn't necessarily mean we won't witness it, endure it, perhaps help and witness to others **through** the trials, testing, and wrath. If tribulation and wrath were one in the same, then we wouldn't be appointed to either, but what does God's Word say? Tribulation and wrath are two separate events with specific meanings and purposes. It's encouraging to know "... God has not appointed us to wrath" (1 Thes 5:9)! It's not our appointment, but we can and may go along, see it, watch it, and go through it - be protected through it.

The Bible does state we are appointed to affliction (1 Thes 3:3) and "we should **suffer tribulation**" (1 Thes 3:4 - trial, testing). Understand that some died and some will die for Christ, but there is a difference between dying for Christ and "wrath" which has an eternity of hell accompanying it. We know God is the same yesterday, today, and tomorrow (Heb 13:8; Ps 102:27; Mal 3:6; Jas 1:17). Since He is the same, let's have a look at history to see what God did, to see any patterns that may help us to understand what's coming. God's faithful went through, endured, and witnessed tribulation (trials, testing, suffering ...) and wrath yet were protected, not destroyed:

1. Noah **persevered through** the 120 years of building the ark, experiencing ridicule and judgment of others, **endured** and witnessed the flood, but was not

destroyed like everything else was. Noah was protected (Gen 7-10; Luke 17:26-27; 2 Pet 2:5).

2. Lot **endured through** the trial, destruction of Sodom and Gomorrah, and was **protected**. God was even willing to save Lot's wife until she was disobedient, and looked back. There is lots more (pun intended) to this fascinating study (Gen 19; Luke 17:26-33; 2 Pet 2:6; Jude 1:7).

3. Daniel **endured** the trial of the lions den but was **protected** from destruction/wrath (Dan 6).

4. Shadrach, Meshach and Abednego went **through** the trial, testing, and wrath of the fiery furnace. They **endured**, and were not destroyed. They, too, were **protected** (Dan 3).

5. Jesus suffered crucifixion and physical death, but was spared and **not destroyed** from a spiritual death. Not only that, He was exalted to Most High. God didn't keep Christ from tribulation (trials/tests). If God wouldn't spare His own Son from tribulation, let alone everyone else who has lived before us, what makes you think He would spare you (us) from tribulation? (Ps 66:10-12; Isa 43:2, 48:10-11; Zec 13:9; 1 Pet 1:6-7;

2 Pet 2:4-10; Dan 3:25-27; Luke 17:26-33; 1 Cor 3:13-17; 2 Thes 1:4; Jas 1:2-4; Jude 1:5,7)

Who was NOT spared?

- The angels that sinned (2 Pet 2:4).
- The world of the ungodly via the flood (2 Pet 2:5; Luke 17:26-33).
- The cities of Sodom and Gomorrah (2 Pet 2:6; Luke 17:24-33; Jude 1:7).

See a pattern? Hmm, let's see ... God tested them. God brings His righteous people through tribulation (trials and/or testing) and through wrath, since they were not "appointed to wrath" (keeps them from wrath, Isa 43:2; 1 Pet 1:6-7). They were protected, not destroyed. So will we escape the seven year Tribulation? Will He test us? If God really is the same yesterday, today, and tomorrow ... and His other obedient believers had to endure through trials, then how could we escape them? Why would we? Would God let us escape and not them? Remember, what is the purpose of trials and testing? Is it not to strengthen our faith, prove it genuine, and to mature us to be more like Christ? What is the purpose of suffering? "... We are to share in the suffering in order to share in His glory ..." (Rom 8:17). We see in

21

Rev 3, it says to hold fast so no one can deceive you and no man take your crown ... **Him that overcome** ... (Rev 3:5, 10-13, 21:7). See what's promised? But we need to overcome, endure. Answer me this! If previously raptured, what is there to overcome? Be encouraged and have faith!!! If, I repeat, if we are not "raptured" pretribulation, God will help us get **through** the tribulation, trials, and wrath. Just like He did then, He does today, and He will do tomorrow (1 Cor 10:13; 2 Pet 2:9)!!

Taken Out of the Way

What exactly does that mean, "... taken out of the way"? Prior to or at the beginning of the Seven Year Tribulation period, some believe the Holy Spirit will be "gone", their understanding of "... taken out of the way." God's Word says in 2 Thes 2:7, "For the mystery of iniquity doth already work: only he who now letteth will let, until he be taken out of the way." Since it's understood we won't be here on earth without the Holy Spirit (Comforter) as Jesus promised, some conclude the church (believers) must be raptured/gone if the Holy Spirit is "gone." John 14:16-17 says, "And I will pray the Father, and he shall give you another Comforter, that he may abide with you for ever; Even the Spirit of truth; whom the world cannot receive, because it seeth him not, neither knoweth him: but ye know him; for he dwelleth with you, and shall be in you." (Also see John 16:7).

Think about it! Is the Holy Spirit gone or perhaps simply removed, set aside, or taken out of the way? How could the Holy Spirit be gone when the believers are still here? Or are they? Does it say they went with Him? If while walking down a path, could you remove an obstacle, say a large branch, from the path and set it aside so you could get by? Would the branch then be "gone" or perhaps just "... taken out of the way"? The Holy Spirit can't be "gone" (therefore, us gone too) prior to the Seven Year Tribulation for four reasons:

1. Remember what the purpose of the Tribulation period is? It is to get the Jews to recognize that Jesus is the Messiah they've been waiting for. Up to this point, the Jews haven't done this and aren't on board yet. Christ is coming back for the church body which consists of both Jews and Gentiles. 1 Cor 12:13 says, "For by one Spirit are we all baptized into one body, whether we be Jews or Gentiles, whether we be bond or free; and have been all made to drink into one Spirit." Furthermore, John 10:16 says, "And other sheep I have, which are not of this fold: them also I must bring, and they shall hear my voice; and there shall be **one** fold, and one shepherd." (Eph 2:11-22). Would Christ take the legs and arms (Gentiles) and leave the trunk of the body (Jews)? I don't think so! The Jews need to accept Christ in order to have the whole body, one body, join Him (Gal 3:28-29; Eph 2:16, 3:6; Isa 56:8, 11:12).

2. If the Holy Spirit is gone, how do those remaining on earth come to accept Christ during the seven years of Tribulation? Or can they? The Holy Spirit has to be

present to bring anyone to repentance. The Holy Spirit will abide with us forever (John 14:16-17) ... never leave us. So, if the Holy Spirit is gone, then we're gone, and no one else can accept Christ as their Savior ... no new believers (1 Cor 2:14, 1:18). Wait a minute!!! That contradicts God's Word. Mercifully, God gives all up through the fifth vial to repent ... that's seven seals, seven trumpets and up to five of seven vials to repent (Rev 16:10-11). On a timeline, that's almost the entire Seven Year Tribulation period to repent. Wow! Is the Holy Spirit gone? According to God's Word, it just can't be. So I ask you, how then could we be gone?

3. Scripture says the Antichrist has to be revealed **before** Christ returns (2 Thes 2:3-4). When is the Antichrist revealed? Scripture says not until the mid (3 ½ yrs. into the tribulation - study abomination of desolation – Dan 9:24-27). So can and will Christ return prior to the middle of the Seven Year Tribulation? Not according to scripture! If we are raptured pretribulation, as some believe, and the Antichrist hasn't been revealed yet, then where are we? What are we doing for 3 ½ years? What proof or scripture is there to back this up? There isn't! God's Word says we'll be changed in the twinkling of an eye at the last trumpet (1 Cor 15:52) ... a far cry from 3 1/2 years. There also needs to be a "falling away first".

The word falling, see the Strong's Concordance, means "defection from truth, forsake, divorce". Remember the fallen angels? Were they not angels that defected from the truth? Check this out ... 2 Thes 2:3 says, "Let no man deceive you by any means: for that day shall not come, except there come a falling away first, and that man of sin be revealed, the son of perdition." Now, insert the meaning of "falling" back into its place in this scripture and what do you get? For example, "... for that day shall not come, except there come a defection from truth first ...". Let me ask you this. Who will fall away? Can non-believers fall way? What would they fall away from? How could they "fall away", choose to walk away from the Lord, if they haven't accepted Christ in the first place? Since non-believers can't fall away, then that leaves who? Only believers! Jesus said, "He who is not with me is against me ..." (Matt 12:30; Luke 11:23). Yikes! Therefore, those falling away will be some believers. If the believers are "gone", raptured pretrib, these scriptures don't line up. How could there be a falling away first, believers defect from the truth, if the believers are already gone? Don't forget, the Antichrist has to be revealed **before** Christ returns. Remember, we are changed in the twinkling of an eye, immediately, and come back with Jesus so if raptured pretrib, there is a 3 ½ year gap of time until the Antichrist is revealed which again happens before Christ returns. Think about it … this just doesn't compute.

4. In addition, think about this! God's Word says, "… and power was given unto him (Antichrist) **to continue** forty and two months" (Rev 13:5). That's 3 ½ years! Although he is here, he isn't revealed until half way through the Tribulation, thus able "to continue forty and two months". That means the Antichrist will be here for the remaining 3 ½ years of the Tribulation. So what will he be doing? Besides blaspheming God, "and it was given unto him to make war with the saints, and to overcome them …" (Rev 13:6-7). Did you get that? First of all, "… it was **given** unto him." Hmm, think about that! Next, who will the Antichrist make war with? The saints! Yikes, that's us believers! Those believers that didn't choose to fall away first. Simply put, if the saints are gone, how can he make war? Not only are we not gone, but we are going to be at war with the Antichrist whose purpose here is to overcome us. Rev 13:5-7 says, "And there was given unto him a mouth speaking great things and blasphemies; and power was given unto him to continue forty and two months. And he opened his mouth in blasphemy against God, to blaspheme his name, and his tabernacle, and them that dwell in heaven. And it was given unto him to make war with the saints, and to overcome them: and power was given

27

him over all kindreds, and tongues, and nations." Getting a little personal? You bet!

Therefore, the church can't be "gone" yet, and the Holy Spirit is "... taken out of the way" (set aside but not "gone" entirely) so that the Antichrist can be revealed. Those remaining have a chance to repent up to the fifth vial, and the rest of prophecy will be fulfilled before Christ returns (2 Thes 2:3-7).

From all we've learned thus far, let's go back and lay out some key points made in scripture on a time line ... see the "Seven Year Tribulation Time Line" as follows:

A) We know the Antichrist is revealed midway through the Tribulation (Dan 9:24-27; Rev 13:5, study abomination of desolation for more scripture references).
B) According to scripture, the Antichrist has to be revealed **before** Christ returns (2 Thes 2:3-4), therefore, Christ can't come before the 3 ½ year mark.
C) The Antichrist will war and overcome the saints for 3 ½ years (Rev 13:5-7).
D) We know God doesn't want any to perish (John 3:16, 6:40; 2 Pet 3:9) and He gives all up through the fifth

28

vial to repent (Rev 16:10-11) so some will accept Christ and become believers during the seven years of Tribulation. Gentle reminder, the Holy Spirit must be present to do so.

Seven Year Tribulation Time Line

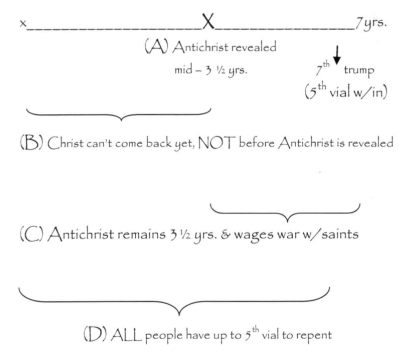

x_____X_____7yrs.

(A) Antichrist revealed
mid – 3 ½ yrs.

7th trump
(5th vial w/in)

(B) Christ can't come back yet, NOT before Antichrist is revealed

(C) Antichrist remains 3 ½ yrs. & wages war w/saints

(D) ALL people have up to 5th vial to repent

To further emphasize that there will be believers during this time, 1 Thes 4:16-17 says, "we which are alive and remain shall be caught up ... in the clouds, to meet the Lord ...". Where does this go on the time line? At the "trump of God" (1 Thes 4:16 - study last day/7ᵗʰ trump). So, if we're raptured pretribulation, there would be no believers here ... no one who was "alive and remain" in order to be caught up at the trump of God. If we are out of here, why does God call for patience and faith of the saints (Rev 13:5-10, Rev 14:1-12)? If raptured **prior** to the 7ᵗʰ trumpet, occurring at the last day, then where are we? "No man was able to enter into the temple, till the seven plagues of the seven angels were fulfilled" (Rev 15:8). For further study, when does that occur? To see God's bigger picture, add that to the time line.

Since we will be changed immediately (1 Cor 15:51-54; Phil 3:21; 1 John 3:2), looking at our time line, does it stand to reason that we are raptured out, changed, seven years go by, then we return with Christ? How does seven years translate to "in a moment, in the twinkling of an eye?" Where are we and what are we doing for those seven years? Scripture doesn't seem to answer those questions. Hmm ... wonder why? Perhaps ... because we aren't out of here yet. Question, when are we changed? When will we be raised up? God's Word says, "at the last

30

trump ... " (1 Cor 15:52) which is the seventh trumpet (Rev 11:15-18), after seven seals and six trumpets. Keep in mind, the seventh trumpet has seven vials, occurring at "the last day", when we're raised up (John 6:39-40). How many "last" days will there be? Hence the word "last," just one!

Remember, what is God's desire? That none shall perish. Christ is coming back for the church body which consists of both Jews and Gentiles ... **one** body (1 Cor 12:13; Eph 2:11-22; John 10:16). Again, God gives all up through the 5th vial to repent. His believers and Holy Spirit are here on earth to endure to the end and to complete our mission of spreading the gospel. Matt 24:13-14 says, "But he that shall endure unto the end, the same shall be saved. And this gospel of the kingdom shall be preached in all the world for a witness unto all nations; and then shall the end come" (Matt 10:22; Mark 13:13).

A Twist? A Twist!

Let us reconsider what is being said in 2 Thessalonians 2: 3-12. Take a moment now to ask Holy Spirit to reveal God's truth and reread this passage.

Now, who is being talked about here? Who is referred to as: that man of sin, the son of perdition, the mystery of iniquity, wicked? Is that not the Antichrist? This whole section emphasizes who he claims to be, his deception and workings, his destiny "whom the Lord shall consume with the spirit of his mouth, and shall destroy with the brightness of his coming" (vs. 8), yet ... there is an appointed time in which he will then be revealed.

Consider an interesting twist. Follow me on this! What if it's not Holy Spirit "... taken out of the way", but perhaps the Antichrist? Again, we are not necessarily talking gone, absent completely, but set aside, out of the way temporarily. Ask yourself what would be the purpose in moving the Antichrist aside?"

Contemplate this! We know God gives power to the two witnesses, and they prophesy 1,260 days (Rev

11:3). That is exactly 3 ½ years. Keep in mind the calendar back then varied from our current 365 day calendar (a revealing study for another time). Next question, when do they receive this power? Scripture doesn't tell us outright as that would be too easy. Once again, we have to dig for it. Get out your shovels, here we go! "And when they shall have finished their testimony, the beast that ascendeth out of the bottomless pit shall make war against them, and shall overcome them, and kill them" (Rev 11:7). Reading through verse 14, we see that the two witnesses will be dead in the street 3 ½ days, followed by other pertinent events which indicates a specific time for us to mark on the time line. This wraps up what is called the second woe, right before the 7th angel sounds the 7th trumpet (Rev 11:14-15). In other words, this occurs in the 6th trumpet. For those of you who may not have studied The Book of Revelation yet, God's Word tells us that the 7th trumpet occurs after the 1st through seven seals, and the seven trumpets are contained in that 7th seal. It also reveals there are seven vials contained in the 7th trumpet (see diagram, next page). Keep in mind, exact time allotments designated to each seal, trumpet, vial, or event are not clearly defined. God's Word does tell us the order in which they take place and their overall total duration, seven years.

34

Seven Year Tribulation Timeline

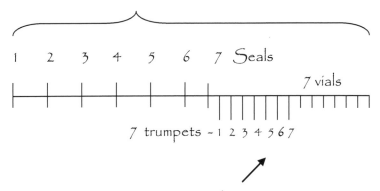

2 witnesses killed @ 6th trumpet ~ Rev 11:7-14

The purpose of this and other diagrams are to give us an easy to comprehend visual aide of God's events to come. Note the 7th seal contains seven trumpets and it, in turn, contains seven vials (Rev 6-16).

As you read, you will see that the two witnesses will be killed near the end of the seven years: the end of the 6th trumpet, just before the 7th trumpet. See that marked on the time line?

Since we are told when they will die, we can figure out approximately when they will arrive on the scene. Scripture tells us they prophesy for 1,260 days. Counting back from their deaths and ascension (6th

trumpet, Rev 11:12-15), it puts their arrival and the power they will have while on earth into play at approximately the 3 ½ year mark, mid point, of the Seven Year Tribulation period.

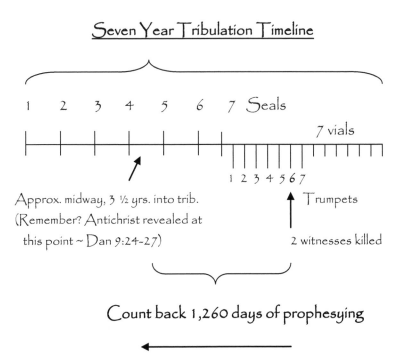

Seven Year Tribulation Timeline

1   2   3   4   5   6   7 Seals

7 vials

1 2 3 4 5 6 7

Approx. midway, 3 ½ yrs. into trib.
(Remember? Antichrist revealed at
this point ~ Dan 9:24-27)

Trumpets

2 witnesses killed

Count back 1,260 days of prophesying

Again, we don't know exactly how long each seal, trumpet, vial, and event will take. Some may be quick, Lord willing, and others may be prolonged. We do know the overall time is seven years and from there we estimate the half way point, 3 ½ years, when the Antichrist is revealed (Dan 9:24-27). Keep in mind, when converting years into days, the calendar then was a 360 day calendar whereas ours today is 365 days. Or is it? Don't forget leap year! Anyhow, it will get you real close. Do you think it's a coincidence that the witnesses arrive in close proximity to when the Antichrist is revealed? Something else to ponder!

Back to our earlier question, what would be the reason to put the Antichrist aside? If he is still on the scene while the two witnesses are prophesying, you may conclude he'd use his power and cause havoc for, or even eliminate, the witnesses. The problem with this is scripture says they are not killed <u>until</u> they "have finished their testimony, the beast ... shall make war against them, and shall overcome them, and kill them" (Rev 11:7). Could it be that God allows the Antichrist back into action at that time, to kill the two witnesses? There is a specific job they are assigned to do with a predetermined time line attached. Not only that, still in reference to the witnesses, "And if any man will hurt them, fire proceedeth out of their mouth, and devoureth their enemies: and if any man will hurt them, he must in this manner be killed" (Rev 11:5). The Antichrist is a man, empowered by Satan, is he not? We see there is a specific plan of action declared in anticipation of any that come against the witnesses, resulting in sure, painful, and physical death. We also know it's not the two witnesses that get the pleasure or responsibility of destroying the enemy, and now is not yet his time of destruction.

What if ... the Antichrist, not the Holy Spirit, is taken out of the way of only the two witnesses, not out of the way of everybody else? Scripture makes it real clear that the Antichrist will be around. "Power was given unto him to continue forty and two months" (Rev 13:5, 3 ½ years, and we know per scripture when his identity is revealed). God's Word goes on to say, "... It was given him to make war with the saints ... overpower them ... over all kindreds, and tongues, and nations ... shall worship him ..." (Rev 13:5-10). Yet, we've already seen that God has a divine plan and purpose for the two witnesses and the Antichrist cannot harm them until the designated time. Take note of Rev 11:7 one more time: "And when they shall have finished their testimony, the beast that ascendeth out of the bottomless pit shall make war against them, and shall overcome them, and kill them." When does the Antichrist kill them? After they have finished their testimony they will be killed (6th trumpet). Where will the Antichrist be coming from? He ascendeth out of the bottomless pit. Wow! Wait a minute! If he comes out of the bottomless pit, how did he get there in the first place? How long has he been there? Could being in the bottomless pit, since that is where he will be ascending from, possibly be considered set aside for a time ... taken out of the way perhaps? This scripture reveals much, and we clearly see his assignment here ... to kill the two witnesses.

Remember, the purpose of the two witnesses is to prophesy for their assigned 1,260 days, to be killed, their dead bodies to be displayed in the street for 3 ½ days, to be witnessed by the entire world, and "ascend up to heaven in a cloud; and their enemies beheld them" (Rev 11:12).

Could the two witnesses possibly fulfill their assignment, not be harmed until the God appointed time, *and* the Antichrist still exercise his God given power and authority over the rest of the world? Taken out of the way? A bit twisted perhaps ... a bit perplexed, but God's ways are not our ways. All that being said, who does God say will be taken out of the way?

For Further Study:

- What does Dan 12:11 reveal regarding the days remaining?

- How many days do the saints need to wait and persevere through, and what is the reward? (Dan 12:12, Rev 13:10)

- What do you suppose is going on during those extra days? When might they occur? (30 days more than the witnesses ... before they appear or after their deaths and ascension? Or ...?)

- Why would there be 45 more days of waiting and enduring? Or will there be?

- Who will those two mystery men witnesses be? Hmm! That's a whole other exciting study.

The Harvest

Let's take a look at Matthew 13:24-30. It says, "Another parable put he forth unto them, saying, The kingdom of heaven is likened unto a man which sowed good seed in his field: But while men slept, his enemy came and sowed tares among the wheat, and went his way. But when the blade was sprung up, and brought forth fruit, then appeared the tares also. So the servants of the householder came and said unto him, Sir, didst not thou sow good seed in thy field? from whence then hath it tares? He said unto them, An enemy hath done this. The servants said unto him, Wilt thou then that we go and gather them up? But he said, Nay; lest while ye gather up the tares, ye root up also the wheat with them. Let both grow together until the harvest: and in the time of harvest I will say to the reapers, Gather ye together first the tares, and bind them in bundles to burn them: but gather the wheat into my barn."

Let's take a closer look at this passage. What was the response given to the servant after he inquired about gathering them up, them being both the tares and the wheat? It was instructed to him, "Let both grow together until the harvest." Secondly, "Gather ... bind in bundles to

burn them (the tares): but gather the wheat into my barn."
(Matt 13: 30) Note the order of events and to whom this
will happen. "Let both grow together **until** the harvest."
(Matt 13:30) Grow how? Together! For how long do
they grow? **Until** the harvest! Hmm, now we have to figure
out when and/or what is the harvest? Thankfully, our
gracious and merciful God clearly tells us.

Now, continue studying Matt 13:36-43 which
explains Matthew 13:24-30, the previous passage, and
tells us definitively about the harvest (also see Rev 14:14-
20).

Matt 13:36-43 says, "Then Jesus sent the
multitude away, and went into the house: and his disciples
came unto him, saying, Declare unto us the parable of the
tares of the field. He answered and said unto them, He
that soweth the good seed is the Son of man; The field is
the world; the good seed are the children of the kingdom;
but the tares are the children of the wicked one; The
enemy that sowed them is the devil; **the harvest is the end
of the world**; and the reapers are the angels. As therefore
the tares are gathered and burned in the fire; so shall it be
in the end of this world. The Son of man shall send forth
his angels, and they shall gather out of his kingdom all
things that offend, and them which do iniquity; And shall

cast them into a furnace of fire: there shall be wailing and gnashing of teeth. Then shall the righteous shine forth as the sun in the kingdom of their Father. Who hath ears to hear, let him hear."

Matt 13:39 says, "...the harvest is the end of the world..." In other words, the tares (children of the wicked one/non-believers) and the wheat (believers) will live together until the end of the world. Wow, let that sink in a minute!

If we are raptured and the nonbelievers have seven more years on earth, how is that both growing/living together until the harvest, the end of the world? Remember, Matt 13:30 says, "Let both grow together until the harvest ..." at which time Jesus gives His command to His angels to gather and separate the tares from the wheat.

Let's take a closer look at the remainder of Matt 13:30: "... and in the time of harvest I will say to the reapers, Gather ye together first the tares, and bind them in bundles to burn them: but gather the wheat into my barn." Jesus tells His angels to gather first the tares (nonbelievers), bind them to burn them but gather the wheat (believers) into His barn. Who is gathered first?

43

The tares, non-believers, are gathered first ... not the wheat . . . not the believers! Why? Why? Why did Jesus tell the angels to gather the tares first? Hmm! Remember what He said "... Bind them in bundles to burn them." Notice the sequence of events. Note the command wasn't given to burn them, but to first bind them in preparation of burning them. The wheat, believers, are then to be gathered. The burning hasn't occurred yet. We believers are gathered, safely protected and brought into His barn, before the tares are burned.

Think about this ... If we are gone/raptured, wouldn't that mean we were gathered first instead of the tares? Something else to think about ... why would Jesus tell His angels to gather us into His barn if we were previously raptured? Wouldn't we already be there or be somewhere with Him? If that's the case, there would be no need to gather and separate us from the tares let alone put us in His barn. Do you see where this is going? Better yet, can you see what God is saying?

As a Thief in the Night

Is Jesus coming as a thief in the night? The Bible says, "For yourselves know perfectly that the day of the Lord so cometh as a thief in the night. For when they shall say, Peace and safety; then sudden destruction cometh upon them, as travail upon a woman with child (once it starts, there's no stopping it ... and it increases); and they shall not escape" (1 Thes 5:2-3).

Since God is the same yesterday, today, and tomorrow, where else in God's Word has this happened, "Peace and safety; then sudden destruction"? Remember the flood in Noah's day and Sodom and Gomorrah? Great examples! Now let's do some more scripture digging! Who are "they" and "them" that 1 Thes 5:2-3 refers to "... sudden destruction cometh upon them ... and they shall not escape." Let's look at who didn't escape. In both examples, the wicked, nonbelievers, those not "righteous" in God's eyes, not walking the walk, did not escape the sudden destruction. So who did survive (escaped **through**) back then? Those who chose to love, follow, and/or <u>obey</u> God. Those who endured were protected and kept from destruction (wrath – chapter 2).

So who will survive in the future? According to 1 Thes 5:4, "But ye, brethren, are not in darkness, that that day should overtake you as a thief." We believers are not in darkness. Let's think about this. Who gets taken over by a thief? Isn't it those who don't watch or prepare? Would a thief come and enter your home to rob it if he knew you were watching, waiting, prepared in case of an unexpected invasion? Hmm! Matt 24:43 says, "But know this, that if the goodman of the house had known in what watch the thief would come, he would have watched, and would not have suffered his house to be broken up."

Another point to ponder ... just how does a thief come? Would it be fair to say a thief comes suddenly, quickly, unexpectedly just as the flood did in Noah's day to those not watching, not prepared, or to those that chose not to obey God? Will Christ's return be a surprise to us like a thief overtaking us in the night would be? It certainly could be, but not if we are watching and prepared. Christ's return will be a surprise to those not watching, like it was for the people in Noah's day or in Sodom and Gomorrah. How about the "casual Christians" today who haven't been, currently aren't, or don't know what to watch for? Will they be surprised? Will you?

Let's dig deeper. The Bible says, "But the day of the Lord will come as a thief in the night; in the which the heavens shall pass away with a great noise, and the elements shall melt with fervent heat, the earth also and the works that are therein shall be burned up." (2 Pet 3:10) What? The earth shall be burned up? Is this not destruction (wrath)? When does this happen? Scripture states it happens when the day of the Lord comes. So ... when is that? The day of the Lord is another way of saying when Christ returns (also refer back to "The Harvest" chapter). Let's think about that for a moment! If Christ returns and we are already "raptured" and God brings **sudden destruction,** (1 Thes 5:2-3), **melting the earth** (2 Pet 3:10), then how could there possibly be anything to come back to, let alone anything or anyone surviving? What about those remaining through the seven years of Tribulation that is talked about throughout His Word? What about God giving all people up to the fifth vial to repent? (Rev 16:10-11) It doesn't make sense! Nor does it line up with the rest of God's Word. Or will Christ come a third time? Scripture does not indicate that either. The pretribulation time line, therefore, needs to be revisited.

To Watch or Not to Watch ...

Referring back to chapter 2, let's recall the definition of tribulation ... trials, testing. With that, if we are "raptured" before tribulation (trials and testing), what should we be watching and preparing for? Why watch or prepare at all since we are out of here, right? What would be the point of God telling us over and over again to watch and prepare? Why would God warn us to guard against being deceived? But ... what if we are here a while longer, perhaps having to go **through** a portion of the Seven Year Tribulation (trial/testing) and possibly wrath? Just as so many others have endured in the past, wouldn't that be something God might want us to watch out for ... and be prepared for ? Did He not warn Noah, Lot, and many others of what's to come? God being the same yesterday, today, and tomorrow, wouldn't He then warn and help us? His Word says we will be tested, persecuted, afflicted, oppressed ... (see ref. in definition of tribulation section – chapter 2). It also says we need to "watch", we believers are not appointed to wrath (destruction, 1 Thes 5:1-11, again not our appointment, but conceivably we may have to go through it). If we're watching, it won't be a surprise to us, and we will be prepared for it when Christ returns.

What if we don't watch? Rev 3:3-5 says, "... If therefore thou shalt not watch, I will come on thee as a thief, and thou shalt not know what hour I will come upon thee." (also Matt 24:42) In other words, if we don't watch, Jesus' coming will be a surprise to us ... suddenly, quickly, unexpectedly ... catching us off guard, perhaps unprepared, as a thief does to his victim. Think about this! What else might this passage be implying? If we were to watch, might we see the signs unfold and know not only what to expect, in what order they are to occur (as He does reveal it to us), but perhaps we would have a better indication of the approximate season or year of His coming? God's Word says in Matt 25:13, "Watch therefore, for ye know neither the **day nor** the **hour** wherein the Son of man cometh" (Matt 24:42) but ... He leaves us clues to find out other pertinent information (another fascinating study). I don't know about you, but I want to prepare, anticipate, and watch for His arrival expectantly, cheering our Lord on as He comes to get us.

Now let's think about who isn't watching. We know nonbelievers are definitely not watching! So, who is supposed to watch? You got it, us believers! But are all believers watching for Christ's return? Didn't Jesus not only tell His disciples to watch, but then question them for not watching? (Matt 26:38-50) He being the same yesterday, today, and tomorrow (Heb 13:8), wouldn't He question us if we don't watch? Here's your challenge should you choose to accept it ... How many times does God tell us in His Word to watch? And prepare? Keep in mind, here is another clue, praying is part of the preparation.

Do "all" believers know what to watch for? Let's get a little personal ... do **you** know what to watch for? Might we be more prepared if we pray, and study to show ourselves approved unto God? His Word specifically says, "Study to shew thyself (show yourself) approved unto God, a workman that needeth not to be ashamed, rightly dividing the word of truth" (2 Tim 2:15). Note that we are to study to show ourselves approved unto God, not unto man. Nowhere does it say to get man's approval as man's approval is only temporary and has no eternal value. It's God's approval we need to seek and gain.

<u>Why should we watch?</u> Here are six reasons, perhaps you'll have more:

1) <u>OBEDIENCE</u> ~ God told us to (Gen-Rev, Matt 24:42-43, 25:13; Mark 13:32-37... obey and remain faithful, Rev 14:12, 13:10).

51

2) <u>TO BE PREPARED</u> for what God tells us is coming (see the "Quick Reference Index" in the back).

3) So we are <u>NOT DECEIVED</u> as "... that day (the day Christ returns) shall <u>not</u> come, except there come a falling away first" (2 Thes 2:3). Again, let me ask you this. Who will fall away? Can nonbelievers fall way? What would they fall away from? How could they "fall away", choose to walk away from the Lord, if they haven't accepted Christ in the first place? Therefore, those falling away will be some believers. Perhaps the ones not watching? Might they be more easily deceived if they don't know what to watch for or aren't prepared? Yikes! Good reason to watch. Let's not be in that group!!!

4) <u>WORTHY TO ESCAPE</u> ~ Luke 21:36 says, "Watch ye therefore, and pray always, that ye may be accounted worthy to escape all these things that shall come to pass, and to stand before the Son of man."

5) <u>TO BE BETTER EQUIPPED</u>, more effective, witnesses for Christ ... better able to share the love of Jesus with others, and help them through, since we know what is coming.

6) <u>TO BE BLESSED</u> ~ Rev 16:15 says, "Behold, I come as a thief. Blessed is he that watcheth ..." Let me ask, if you are watching, are you not better prepared? If you think a thief might be coming, would you be watching out for him? Would you prepare so that he couldn't steal from you? Would you lock your doors, leave lot's of lights on, stay up and stand guard, perhaps even alert the police? Watching, and praying, are part of the preparation, so those who watch and prepare are blessed ... Jesus says so.

To quickly recap, we see six vital reasons why watching certainly would be beneficial to say the least. I can think of several reasons why not watching would undoubtedly be an unwise, possibly eternity impacting, choice. We see what God says. Now, what do you say? To watch or not to watch?

"What If"

Seriously consider...

What if you believe in the **pretribulation** rapture of the church and it **_is_ true**? Praise the Lord ... we are out of here! No enduring intense trials, testings, or going through, part or all, of the seven years of Tribulation. No need to watch or prepare. We got off easy. Thank you Jesus.

What if you believe in the **pretribulation** rapture and it is **_not_ true**? What do you do, not knowing what is coming next or what to watch and prepare for? What does that say to all those who trusted or believed "Christians" of the pretribulation rapture belief, and now they find out that pretribulation is not so (it did not happen)? Is the rest of Christian faith inaccurate and also perhaps a lie? This would not be a good situation to have to explain to those we've witnessed to. If you don't know what to watch and prepare for, might there be a better chance that you could be more easily deceived? Remember, there will be a falling away first. God says so! (2 Thes 2:3; 2 Pet 3:17)

What if you believe mid or post-trib, pre-wrath or even post wrath rapture and it is ***not* true**? Praise the Lord! What have you lost other than perhaps some "time" in the Word preparing, studying, learning what to watch for, strengthening and deepening your personal relationship with the Lord. Shouldn't we be doing that anyway? (2 Tim 2:15...)

What if you believe mid or post-trib, pre-wrath or post wrath rapture of the church and it ***is* true**? Then what? You'll be prepared and know exactly what to watch for. Do you know the Lord may use you in those circumstances ... His prepared, watchful, righteous, obedient, blessed servants? You Bet! How exciting!

Now, what are we to watch for? Pray and read Matt 24; Luke 21; Mark 13 to get started, followed by 2 Pet 3:17; Rev 3:2-5, 16:15; 1 Thes 5:6; 2 Thes 2:3-4; 2 Tim 3:1-5; Ezekiel 7... and more. Hey, you didn't really think I was going to make it easy by telling you ... or did you? Read and compare. Cross reference. Dig, dig, dig, there's lot's more to watch for! This is the one time you do not want to procrastinate and you do not want to be left out!

<u>When does Christ return?</u> For that answer, I suggest you do a time line and lot's of reading and comparing. God is faithful as He **does** tell us in His Word, not the day or the hour, yet everything else like the order and season (s) in which things and events must and will take place ... but we have to work for it and dig for it (study to show ourselves approved). It's certainly worth it and real exciting! Hint, start digging at: Matt 24; Luke 17, 21; Mark 13; Dan 9; 1 Thes 4 & 5; 2 Thes 2; Rev 3, 6, ... , 16, 21 just for starters and more throughout God's Word. I suggest you expand the time line that we have already established showing the seven seals, seven trumpets, and seven vials (see chapter 4). Include the pertinent points of A and B found in the first time line (see chapter 3). Again, this will help you visualize when Christ can't come back, ruling certain options out, thus narrowing the possibilities. The more you dig and add to your time line, the clearer it becomes, seeing what must happen, and in what order, before Christ will be allowed to return. Again, God tells us, not the day or the hour, but you will get real close and you will know what to watch for. He is faithful as He has provided it for those of us who study to show ourselves approved unto Him.

If for nothing else, I pray this has encouraged you to: dig deeper into God's Word for <u>His truth</u>, desire a more intimate <u>relationship with Jesus</u>, and comfort you in seeing that God will protect and reward His obedient faithful children ... our God is the same yesterday, today, and tomorrow.

Based on God's Word, where do you stand???

What will you do with this knowledge and understanding that the Holy Spirit has revealed?

Are you willing to study to show yourself approved?

Are you willing to work and do what it takes so you know for sure what to be watching for and how to prepare?

My motto is: "Let's pray for the best and prepare for the worst!"

Be Encouraged!

We have had much to think about haven't we? My continued prayer for you is that our Lord Jesus would strengthen and encourage you, build your faith, and bring you to an even deeper, more intimate relationship with Him. What better way than through His Word. Please ... be encouraged!

"For ye have need of patience (persistence), that, after ye have done the will of God, ye might receive the promise. For yet a little while, and he that shall come will come, and will not tarry (delay). Now the just shall live by faith: but if any man draw back, my soul shall have no pleasure in him. But we are not of them who draw back unto perdition (destruction); but of them that believe to the saving of the soul." (Heb 10:36-39)

"He that dwelleth in the secret place of the most High shall abide under the shadow of the Almighty. I will say of the LORD, He is my refuge and my fortress: my God; in him will I trust. Surely he shall deliver thee from the snare of the fowler, and from the noisome pestilence. He shall cover thee with his feathers, and under his wings shalt thou trust: his truth shall be thy shield and buckler.

Thou shalt not be afraid for the terror by night; nor for the arrow that flieth by day; Nor for the pestilence that walketh in darkness; nor for the destruction that wasteth at noonday. A thousand shall fall at thy side, and ten thousand at thy right hand; but it shall not come nigh thee. Only with thine eyes shalt thou behold and see the reward of the wicked. Because thou hast made the LORD, which is my refuge, even the most High, thy habitation; There shall no evil befall thee, neither shall any plague come nigh thy dwelling. For he shall give his angels charge over thee, to keep thee in all thy ways. They shall bear thee up in their hands, lest thou dash thy foot against a stone. Thou shalt tread upon the lion and adder: the young lion and the dragon shalt thou trample under feet. Because he hath set his love upon me, therefore will I deliver him: I will set him on high, because he hath known my name. He shall call upon me, and I will answer him: I will be with him in trouble; I will deliver him, and honour him. With long life will I satisfy him, and shew him my salvation." (Psalm 91)

Remember, be encouraged, and praise God, that we know the end of the story ... "But the saints of the most High shall take the kingdom, and possess the kingdom for ever, even for ever and ever." (Dan 7:18)

Brain Teasers

As you continue studying, try these brain teasers, frequently asked questions, on for size.

Read 1 Thes 4:14-18 ... We're supposed to comfort one another ... how would suffering through the tribulation be of comfort? Now, read through verse 5:11 as his thought isn't completed yet, hence the word "But" in 1 Thes 5:1. We must read through the entire thought for full understanding thus avoiding assumptions or misconceptions. Note 1 Thes 5:4 says, "But ye, brethren, are not in darkness, that that day should overtake (surprise) you as a thief." If we were raptured, why would we need comforting? "Comfort" was for the Thessalonica church because their concern was themselves right then. The comfort for them was that as believers, they will be with the Lord forever (1 Thes 4:17).

Aren't we in a time/period of "grace"? It would be grace to us to be taken up before the tribulation, but not for those who remain. Remember, God wishes that none should perish. Is it not grace that God gives all up through the 5th vial to repent? (2 Pet 3:9; Rev 16:10-11). What amazes me is some still will *choose* not to repent.

How do we follow Jesus out of heaven if we're down on earth? We'll be caught up and changed quickly, in a twinkling of an eye at the last trumpet (refer back to chapters 2 and 3 for further explanation). Changed how? From terrestrial to celestial, incorruptible (1 Thes 4:16-17; 1 Cor 15:51-54; Phil 3:21).

If the Seven Year Tribulation is only for the Jews, what about the Gentiles who want to repent? Aren't they part of the body too? (see chapter 3)

Since the churches aren't talked about after chapter 3 in The Book of Revelation, doesn't that mean they are gone so we are gone (raptured) too? Please be careful not to try and make scripture say something it doesn't (Rev 22:18-19). Just because they aren't talked about again doesn't mean they are raptured. Does scripture say they are gone? The Book of Revelation is not written chronologically. We need other books of the bible to help understand it (compare with i.e.: Daniel, Matt 24, 1 Thes, ...). The Book of Revelation is a vision that jumps back and forth many times even though some segments are in order. For example, the first six seals are listed in order, starting in Revelation chapter 6, and going through the 6th trumpet detailed in chapter 9. Here's an example of scripture out of chronological sequence. It's not until Revelation chapter 11 that we are introduced to the two witnesses, only to find out that they die back in the 6th trumpet, found in Rev 9, and the witnesses actually arrived 1,260 days earlier, Rev 6. In other words, Rev 11 says what they've already done prior to their deaths, counting back 1,260 days (3 ½ yrs.), not telling us earlier when it was going to happen, hence, a flashback (see chapter 4, the time line chart detailing the two witnesses). If The Book of Revelation was written chronologically, their arrival would have been documented in Rev 6, not Rev 11. Keep in mind; this is just one of many examples.

Since the Holy Spirit is omnipresent, isn't it true that He is gone ("taken out of the way" - 2 Thes 2:7) and here on earth at the same time so others can commit to the Lord? First of all, who does scripture say is "taken out of the way"? It doesn't say he's "gone" (refer to chapters 3 and 4). There is a difference! Secondly, scripture doesn't say the Holy Spirit is both gone and here on earth at the same time. Third, Jesus is omnipresent, yet He isn't walking the earth. Remember, Jesus left us His Holy Spirit (counselor – John 14:16, 16:7).

If almost all the disciples were martyred, and God is the same yesterday, today and tomorrow, why wouldn't His disciples of today, or end times, also be martyred?

Digging Deeper

Here's an intriguing research project. I challenge you to dig deeper into God's Word and history.

Has pretribulation rapture always been taught or is it a theory that came about somewhere along the way? If so, how, when and why did it enter the picture? I think if you take the time to research the answers, you will be quite surprised just how recent it is in comparison to our world's history time line (try googling it for starters).

Read Matt 10:22 ~ "And ye shall be hated of all men for my name's sake: but he that endureth to the end shall be saved." Also see Matt 24:13 ~ "But he that shall endure unto the end, the same shall be saved." Follow up with Rev 3, "He that overcometh ..." We will need to overcome something and endure unto the end. Now ask yourself, "Self, is getting out at the beginning of the Seven Year Tribulation *enduring* to the end?" What else could there possibly be to overcome? What will we have to endure unto the end ?

Read Matt 24:22 ~ "And except those days should be shortened, there should no flesh be saved: but for the elect's sake those days shall be shortened." For whose sake will those days be shortened? The elect, the believers! If we weren't here, there would be no reason to shorten them. So why will they be shortened? Perhaps if they aren't shortened, not even the elect will make it, just like God said. Hmm! When will those days be shortened? I encourage you to dig deeper for God's answer and put it on the time line. Tighten your boot straps, it's gonna get tough! But hold on to God's truth and His promises that He is faithful and He will never leave you nor forsake you. Amen!!! (Deut 31:6,8; Jos 1:5; Heb 13:15).

Read Acts 2:20 (vs. 17-21) and put it on the time line. Where does this line up with the same event in The Book of Revelation and when does that occur? Another piece to this puzzle can be found in two books, Revelation and _____? Hint: the other book is in the Old Testament. Where else does scripture talk about the moon turning to blood? Back to Acts 2:20, note the word "before." What **must** take place **before** the Lord comes? See it? When does that happen? He won't come back sooner. Why? His Word says it, and He never contradicts His Word!

Read Rev 15:1 ~ Note the timing and what they are filled with (clue words: last and wrath).

Read Rev 19:7 ~ Study the timing of the wedding of the Lamb and put it on the time line. You just may be surprised!

Read 1 John 3:2 ~ "... when he shall appear, we shall be like him." Think through all we have learned through this study and ask yourself the questions: who, what, where, when, why, and how, amongst any others.

Are you getting some good nuggets? Again, be sure to lay out your findings, God's answers, on the time line. This really helps to have a visual tool and to see God's plan revealed.

A Detailed Big Picture

To gain a much more detailed big picture of what God has revealed to us Saints through His Word, keep that shovel out. I propose an even bigger challenge to you that will amaze you. Keep digging! Put the following verses on the time line, in addition to those we have already done: Acts 2:20 (see previous chapter, "Digging Deeper"); Rev 8:12; Isa 13:10; Matt 24:29; Luke 17:24-33; the seven seals, seven trumpets, and seven vials/bowls found in Rev, Rev 15:1, 16:15 and others the Lord leads you to.

Remember...
"Study to shew thyself (show <u>yourself</u>)
approved unto God."
(2 Tim 2:15)

Now, what will you do
with what God has revealed
to you?

Prayer of Salvation
(Asking Jesus Into Your Heart)

Asking Jesus into your heart is really not as scary as you might think. Doing so will be the most life changing experience you will ever encounter this side of heaven.

As we have done throughout this bible study, let's go back, together, to God's Word for guidance. Remember, it's His ways, not man's, that we are seeking.

First of all, did you know you can't earn or work for your salvation (eternal life) and you can't buy it? Many other "religions" are based on working or earning one's way to heaven, but according to God's Word, it is a gift. "For by grace are ye saved through faith; and that not of yourselves: it is the gift of God: Not of works, lest any man should boast." (Eph 2:8-9) A true gift is given freely, no strings attached, expecting nothing in return. God freely gave His Son Jesus to us (1 Pet 3:18; Rom 5:8). Now, with any gift, we have a **choice** whether or not to receive it. Will you accept His gift? Here's how!

God does not have a set prayer or formula to go by. It's not about saying all the right words; it's about a heart of true repentance, believing, and simply taking a step of faith. God's Word says, "That if thou shalt confess with thy mouth the Lord Jesus, and shalt believe in thine heart that God hath raised him from the dead, thou shalt be saved. For with the heart man believeth unto righteousness; and with the mouth confession is made unto salvation. " (Rom 10:9-10) "If we confess our sins, he is faithful and just to forgive us our sins, and to cleanse us from all unrighteousness." (1 John 1:9)

Just simply talk to God. That's what prayer is. From your heart, admit to God that you are a sinner in need of a Savior, confess, repent, and ask for forgiveness. Declare that you believe Jesus is God's Son, He died for your sins, and rose from the dead. (Rom 3:23; 1 Pet 3:18; Rom 5:8; Isa 53:6; Gal 2:20). Next, give Jesus permission, by asking Him, to come into your heart. That's it! If you <u>chose</u> to do so, you <u>received</u> God's free gift (John 1:12-13, Rom 10:9-10).

Congratulations ! John 1:12-13 says, "But as many as received him, to them gave he power to become the sons of God, even to them that believe on his name: Which were born, not of blood, nor of the will of the flesh, nor of the will of man, but of God." As if that's not enough, since you made that <u>choice</u> to <u>receive</u>, heaven is rejoicing over you (Luke 15).

Welcome to a life with Jesus and the promise of eternity (1 John 5:11-12). Be sure to mark the day as this day is now known as your re-birthday or born again birthday. Now go tell someone and celebrate!

It would be an honor to hear of your commitment to Christ. Please share with me at: www.drinzerillo.com .

Here are other scripture references to affirm your decision in choosing Jesus as your Lord and Savior: Rom 6:23; Gal 2:20; 1 John 5:11-13; John 5:24; 1 Pet 3:18; Matt 24:10-13; Luke 15 ...

QUICK REFERENCE INDEX

Study Notes ~
Getting Ready for the Grand Finale

_____

_____

_____

_____

_____

_____

_____

_____

_____

_____

_____

_____

_____

_____

_____

_____

_____

Study Notes ~
Are Tribulation and Wrath the Same?

Study Notes ~
Taken Out of the Way

Study Notes ~
A Twist? A Twist!

Study Notes ~
The Harvest

Study Notes ~
As a Thief in the Night

_____

_____

_____

_____

_____

_____

_____

_____

_____

_____

_____

_____

_____

_____

_____

_____

Study Notes ~
To Watch or Not to Watch ...

Study Notes ~
What If

Study Notes ~
Be Encouraged!

_____

_____

_____

_____

_____

_____

_____

_____

_____

_____

_____

_____

_____

_____

_____

_____

_____

_____

_____

Study Notes ~
Brain Teasers

_____

_____

_____

_____

_____

_____

_____

_____

_____

_____

_____

_____

_____

_____

_____

_____

_____

_____

_____

_____

_____

Study Notes ~
Digging Deeper

_____

_____

_____

_____

_____

_____

_____

_____

_____

_____

_____

_____

_____

_____

_____

_____

_____

_____

Study Notes ~
A Detailed Big Picture

About the Author

Born and raised in Northern California, D.R. Inzerillo now resides in "the other state," Southern California. After earning a Business Degree in Marketing, pursuing a business career, and marrying the man of her dreams, through a life altering, near death experience, Dodee committed her heart to Jesus Christ, gladly claiming her Christian identity. She was then called to Child Development and Human Relations by way of "Motherhood", through adoption. Shortly thereafter, Educator (including Homeschooling), Writer, and Author were added to her repertoire.

You will soon discover that Dodee is passionate about people. With a heart to encourage, she desires to help others find answers and pursue their dreams. With her love for God's Word, especially Eschatology (study of end times), you'll understand why she was called to write this book, with still more to come. A classically trained scholar, theologian, of formal seminary schooling she is not. But wait . . . neither was Moses the adopted stutterer, King David the once lowly shepherd boy, or Rahab, Jericho's town prostitute, yet God chose them. Dodee does not consider herself to be a mighty leader, of royal stature, or ... She's an ordinary person, chosen by God, for this very reason, as were they, so that God would be magnified. God chose then and still chooses today, ordinary people to do extraordinary things. What assignment does He have you on? In conclusion, D.R. Inzerillo has extensively researched, studied, and/or taught this intriguing subject for more than a decade and sees it as an intricate part of her calling, helping all to watch and prepare for the return of Christ.

It's with a heart of compassion that D.R. Inzerillo invites, encourages, and challenges her readers and everyone to pursue a more intimate relationship with Jesus, dig deeper into His Word, and to seek God's answers, not man's. As she has been known to demonstrate, they are there; you just have to dig for them. In doing so, we will be better equipped to know what to watch for and how to prepare for Christ's return.

Like Rahab, who recognized Almighty God for who He was, knew she wanted to be on His side, was willing to risk her life to help His people, and chose to step out in faith, Dodee reflects the same.

On behalf of Dodee, "thank you" for taking a few minutes of your valuable time to read about her, the woman God has made and called her to be.

Thank you for reading

"The Return of Christ ...
What If"

As you Watch and Prepare, should you desire to "Contact
the Author", or just come discover more,
please visit my Website:

www.drinzerillo.com

Watch the website for more writings including a
rockin', faith based, teacher & student curriculum, targeted
at any group who desire to go through Bible boot camp ...
a Holy Spirit inspired download, tested on home
schoolers and credential teacher approved, its name and
availability are to be unveiled soon.